A DEACON'S RETREAT

Deacon James Keating

Paulist Press
New York/Mahwah, NJ

To Father Richard Gabuzda,
Father John Horn, SJ, and Kathy Kanavy
IN GRATITUDE FOR THEIR FIDELITY
TO THE MINISTRY OF PRIESTLY FORMATION

Cover design by Cynthia Dunne, www.bluefarmdesign.com
Book design by Lynn Else

The cover design of the Clarus Cross with the traditional Deacon's stole is courtesy of Deacon Bill Scarmardo for Pax Creations, Inc., 1-866-779-3336, www.paxcreations.com.

Library of Congress Cataloging-in-Publication Data

Keating, James.
A deacon's retreat / James Keating.
p. cm.
ISBN 978-0-8091-4644-4 (alk. paper)
1. Spiritual retreats for clergy—Catholic Church. 2. Lord's Supper—Meditations. I. Title.
BX1912.5.K43 2010
269'.692—dc22

2009037242

Published by Paulist Press
997 Macarthur Boulevard
Mahwah, New Jersey 07430

www.paulistpress.com

Printed and bound in the United States of America

Contents

Introduction

"Prayer always remains the voice of all those who have no voice—and in this voice there always echoes that 'loud cry' attributed to Christ by the Letter to the Hebrews [5:7]."

—John Paul II, *The Holy Spirit in the Life of the Church and the World*, 1986, n. 65

To enter a retreat as a deacon is to allow one's consciousness to be affected by what Pope John Paul II has written above. The deacon serves the poor through the many ways found in the corporal and spiritual works of mercy; he serves them foremost as *a spiritual man bearing spiritual gifts*. One of the great gifts of the diaconate is given when each man asks Christ for a share in His own cry to the Father, a cry of dependence, love and obedience. The last thing a deacon wants is for his ministry to become a skill and his presence to others to become routine. If we ask Christ for a share in His cry, a share in His own prayer from the depths of His heart, we shall know something of the intimacy He had with the Father. We will also know His death and resurrection.

The prime gift that we give to those to whom we minister Christ is an invitation to receive the love and intimacy willed by God for all His creatures. We are called to accompany people to the very depths of their souls and there encourage them to receive the presence of God over and over. The deepest cry of those we minister to is one that carries the desire to receive God and be received by God. As this desire begins to be satiated, the deacon appears to further accompany each person in the sharing of both food for the souls and food for the body.

For a deacon to enter this retreat he enters his own personal call from God to come and share in Christ's own *eager availability*. Christ is always available to both the Father and to others as His Spirit reaches out to His church. With a new capacity to receive His healing presence, born of prayerful intimacy with Christ, we then render ourselves available to those who cry out day and night for spiritual truth and material welfare. Any diaconal retreat has as its goal the beginning or deepening of a radical availability to the mystery of Christ. This availability in prayer does not simply occur during set prayer times but, by way of this retreat, and continuing daily after its conclusion, such availability fills the *deacon's character*. In so becoming, the deacon no longer lets the occupations of the day become a pretext for denying to Christ the interior intimacy He desires to have with him. In becoming deeply available to Christ, the deacon does not pray and *then* minister; rather, he is *becoming* prayer thus allowing his service to become that of Christ's own. The deacon who allows Christ to reach him in prayer is never separated from Christ.... "And it is no longer I who live, but it is Christ who lives in me" (Gal 2:20). Therefore his ministry is not simply an exercise in competency or virtuous practice but is an *extended presence of his own ongoing communion with Christ in the context of being sent by the Bishop*.

For the structure of our retreat we will meditate upon those parts of the Eucharist that call for diaconal service. As the *National Directory for the Formation, Ministry and Life of the Permanent Deacon* (herein *ND*) noted, "The diaconal spirituality is nourished by the Eucharist, which, not by chance, characterizes the ministry of the deacon" (n. 112). What characterizes our life and ministry is the self-offering of Christ as one who came to *serve*. By contextualizing this retreat within the service rendered at the altar by the deacon we can establish our conversions within the very heart of Christ's own self-offering upon the cross and the Father's response in the resurrection. In other words, as we pray for our own conversion during this retreat we wish to attach our imaginations to the most pivotal event ever to occur in history: the salvation of humankind by way of Christ's obedience to Father, even to His own death. May we realize in gratitude the generous love of God that made this paschal mystery ever available to His church in sacramental form.

This book is **not** meant to be merely read, but is truly meant to be *prayed*. There is no need to rush through it.

You may take a meditation and extend your prayer and contemplation over its content throughout one hour or throughout a week. Whenever you open this book intend to meet God within your heart, because that is the Father's perennial desire. *He desires you*. He wants everlasting communion with you in His Son. Let the meditations of this book give you a deeper prayer life and a deeper receptivity to your own diaconal vocation. Perhaps as you pray this book you will want to have sacred music accompany you, or perhaps you will want to place a crucifix nearby to contemplate, perhaps an open Bible will call to you to come deeper into the original revelation. You may even want to pray this book and have your diaconal stole on your lap using it to bring to mind the generosity of God as he calls you to share in His Son's service. Ultimately, during this retreat let Christ reach you: be available to Him so that He might make you more available to serve the spiritual and charitable needs of His church.

The text of this book is given with one end and one end only: *to mediate the Holy Spirit to your heart. Prayer is the measure of this book and prayer alone*. Prayer is the measure because prayer is the birthplace of charity, and charity is the everlasting goal of our lives in God, and the emblematic service we embody as deacons. Let us begin our retreat, then, by invoking the Holy Spirit:

> *Holy Spirit breathe within our hearts, soften our hardness of heart, our coldness toward your coming. Help us to know the urgency and necessity of our own*

conversions. Plead with us from within; teach us the sound of your voice, the voice of truth, of unity, of holy participation in the love between the Father and the Son. Take us up into that love, and that love alone. And from this share in divine holiness bless our diaconal service. Amen.

May the Spirit be our guide as we prayerfully attend to the following meditations.

Now, let us enter our prayer.

Meditation One

Preparing to Be Affected by Christ

To be a man in the cultural West is to be a man who is somewhat alienated from interior movements of the heart. It is not easy for men to turn inward. Allowing oneself to be affected by interior realities, however, is crucial to diaconal ministry. Deacons have to model lives of interiority for the people they minister to in the diocese. To be a deacon is to be a man called to spiritual living, and not simply one who executes acts of charity. In fact, executing acts of charity disconnected from interior communion with Christ is the surest way for a deacon to taste depression, sadness and apathy. If you are not drawing your ministry from the well of communion with Christ then from what source are you drawing such self-donation? The ego? Your own native wit, natural talent or charisma? If so, such sources of service will soon run dry and your diaconal ministry will not be suited for the long run, but only for sprinting. While praying this retreat just go to God and simply be with Him…without agenda or time lines…just come and sit or kneel despite worries or distractions. "Don't worry," the Spirit says, "*I will come to you*...Prayer is not your work, it is my healing."

First and foremost, the deacon is to be possessed by a spiritual truth; Christ wants communion with you in and by way of the sacramental Church. Such availability to Christ is the key to a faithful and powerful diaconal ministry.

Second, deacons are also men of the Western culture. In general they too are not necessarily comfortable or eager to go into the soul and receive the love of God as the integral power binding the mind, the will and affect all together in Christ. Such a personal encounter can appear to be more threat than promise. Many deacons have made it through their formation process with little or no instruction in deep and sustained prayer. That is also true, regrettably, for some seminarians and priests. The clerical formation system is dominated by academic models of formation and utilitarian models of ministry. We are heady in our understanding of the mystery of Christ, and we are very busy in our understanding of ministry. I would hope that in praying over this retreat you ask for the grace to receive the truths of academic theology as prayer and that you set out to minister in a way that avoids the misconception that prayer is to be left behind in the busy-ness of pastoral concerns. Your ministry IS NOT your prayer but from *within* your ministry Christ emerges to console, challenge and inspire you, and through you others. Alternately, your prayer time is NOT isolated from your desire to labor for the needs of your people. Unless, however, you really make your heart available to God in prayer your presence among the people will simply be clever or virtuous or useful but it will not be holy or healing.

If diaconal ministry is to be fruitful it must flow from our communion with Christ. Interior intimacy with Christ is constitutive of ministry, otherwise we are simply do-gooders. So, we are bid to go in…deeper than you imagine or probably think possible (we are to "pray without ceasing"—1 Thess 5:17). In so doing we can then be sent from Him to serve others, sent not from our ego or even from our good intentions but from Him. We are sent from Him by way of the desires He purifies. We want to serve, He wants to serve within us: *let* Him. This kind of interior life can be understood as that habitual disposition to receive the gift of God's love enabling our capacity for active self-donation.

The spiritual energy for diaconal ministry is found by living dynamically two biblical truths: "It is no longer I who live, but it is Christ who lives in me" (Gal 2:20). And "Here am I; send me!" (Isa 6:8). Diaconal ministry is sustained and deepened at the confluence of interior prayer and the desire to serve the church. When we live our lives as prayer, as a life of a sacred exchange between our freedom and God's own self-offering in Christ, then we begin to move from the mind we have now to a new mind. We allow the mind of Christ to possess us and we begin to think in new ways, we allow Him to "think in us" as Jean Pierre de Caussade radically phrased it.[1] We desire to put

1. Jean Pierre de Caussade, *Treatise on Prayer from the Heart* (St. Louis: Institute of Jesuit Sources, 1998) 145, n. 38.

on the mind of Christ because we have known the darkness of our own minds when they are left to their own self-enclosed ways.

So, there is no true formation as deacons without conversion, and there is no ongoing spiritual ministry after formation without deep attachment to the source of that conversion—the continual reception of the love of God in Christ.

The pathology found in our spiritual lives is always a movement toward isolation and away from this deep interior communion with Christ in the midst of the church. Spiritual sickness originates in keeping the truth about ourselves to or even from ourselves. This is what Satan wants; he always wants us to feel that we are beyond hope, that our problems and sufferings are too deep to be healed. He wants us cornered so he can attack us personally ("you are an immoral man," "you are a sick person," "you are a unique sinner, no one is as bad as you are") and then separate us from hope, to stop our prayer life. Ironically, it is through solitude that such isolation can be *healed*. In solitude we commune with Christ and He leads us to life-giving waters. He names our sins but unlike Satan doesn't besmirch our name. In isolation we suffer the agony of hiding from God in the manner of Adam in the garden. Primarily we hide in desolate affections (self-pity, envy, sadness, unhealed grief) and sin. From such a lonely place a deacon's ministry cannot bear leaves and fruit that heal others (Ezek 47:12). To be spiritual men we must not simply take on a MISSION we must receive the MYSTERY.

It is the MYSTERY, the encounter with and the continual living in the presence of the life, death and resurrection of Christ that gives our ministry evangelical authority. We have a relationship with Christ, he takes us to the Father in the Spirit, thus giving us an identity, and flowing from this identity a mission.

As we continue in the diaconal mission we need to deepen our attention to interiority, to the movements of the Holy Spirit as these are tested in spiritual direction and made clearer in acts of charity and fidelity to family and diaconal life. *Christ lives in us*. This is true, but without vigilance it can simply become another way of approaching the ego. There has to be a real way to distinguish my "I" from the "Thou" which is Christ. If Christ is not other than the ego then we can give up the ministry. His voice is NOT our voice. His voice carries revelation and vocation, our voice consistently carries fears, rationalizations, justification. As we deepen the spiritual life we become attuned to HIS VOICE and HIS ALONE. Analogically this is what happens in an emotionally and spiritually healthy marriage. After a while a spouse learns to listen to his spouse's voice, then her gestures, then he incorporates the beloved's well-being into his conscience so that he knows what actions benefit his wife; this is the level of connatural knowledge. I have internalized my spouse so I know her. I know what to do and how to serve her needs simply as a result of this kind of interior knowing. Is Christ in you as another PERSON? Have you internalized His presence? If you have, then you know Him and you know what to do, because you can

FEEL, you can SENSE His interior movements. You have listened to Him in prayer, in spiritual direction, through revelation, worship and virtuous living, and as a result you have internalized Him. Due to this internalization you can now discern His movements in your life.

In the end, with God's grace, it is up to us to continually choose to stay in His presence. You can *choose to stay in His presence* by the internalizing process that accompanies the following truths: What we think about we become, what we choose we become, what we attend to we become. What we love we become.

If you think about the mystery of Christ you will become that mystery, if you choose to love Christ he will live his life over again in you, if you attend to His Spirit within you then this Spirit will create you anew!

Christ's Spirit is in us to *help* us, not *condemn* us. The Spirit wants to move us deeper and deeper into communion with Christ, purifying us of our affection for sin and giving us the grace to endure our own conversions. The Spirit consoles us and encourages us in and through the power of Christ's own mysteries to never give up, no matter how weary we get, how predictable our falls, how disheartening our own inability to live up to what we believe and preach. The Spirit who lives within us says to us, "surrender, entrust and then receive. Be open; all healing is found in your acceptance of the love of God." The most fruitful human activity is to RECEIVE God.[2]

---

2. Jean Corbon, *The Wellspring of Worship* (San Francisco: Ignatius, 2005), 37.

The *goal* of the spiritual life is ordered toward giving God the core, the heart of who we are. The *work* of the spiritual life is discerning if we have not yet done that fully. God does not want what you give him, primarily He wants you. And alternately, He does not want you to simply receive his gifts but His very being. Is God enough for you? As venerable John Henry Newman pleaded, "Teach me to love prayer, God teach me to love what will occupy my heart for all eternity."[3] By way of moral, intellectual and affective conversion let the Holy Spirit bring Christ to life in your diaconate, in your ministry, and in your hearts...that is the mission of the Holy Spirit.

Because we fear death we fear the spiritual life as it invites us to let God choose for us, let God think for us. Out of fear we hold fast to the fat, relentless ego. We need to seriously consider if we can die to this age before we literally end up dead. We are called to be dead to sin and alive to Christ (Rom 6:11). Until we are *ordered* toward the heart of Christ and what it contains (exclusive and rapt listening to the Father's will) fear and sin will form our minds. *Love alone must form our minds.* What we love always forms our minds. We just have to discern *if* what we are loving now, what we are paying attention to now, is worthy of our dignity.

Take some time now to simply enter the Lord's Presence. Seek to find Him at the core of your heart

3. John Henry Newman, *Meditations and Devotions* (London: Burns and Oates, 1964), 26–7.

and speak to Him honestly about your ideas and feelings around your vocation and prayer life. Listen to His response in the silence of your heart or from praying with scripture. Note any movements within you that signal a healing or a better grasp of how much you are loved by Him. Throughout this retreat utilize a notebook to record the fruit of the experience of your prayer. Such a recording deepens our gratitude toward God because we have a true record of His coming to us and changing us from within.

Now, let us begin our meditation about our vocation as it flows directly from our service at the Eucharist.

Meditation Two
The Penitential Rite

After the deacon processes to the altar with the priest at the beginning of the Eucharist he and the priest kiss the altar. The deacon kisses the place of sacrifice. He directs his body to reverence the place of consecrated self-offering by Christ. In some way the deacon is praying in this kiss the opposite meaning of Judas's kiss. Judas was kissing the Lord in a vile act of betrayal; his openness to being affected by Christ as imaged in a kiss was not genuine. He did not want to be affected by Christ: he wanted to act against what Christ had taught and had been during His ministry. The Judas kiss is a denial of the truth that salvation comes through loving sacrifice.

As deacons we long to kiss the altar in reverence for the sacrifice, we wish to bend to the mystery and allow the Spirit to raise the sacrifice of Christ in all its power and beauty to our minds. "Yes, Lord, I will kiss this stone, this place of unjust killing, this place where previous kisses led to betrayal and not communion. Lord, guide me into the meaning of my kiss, the meaning of my receptivity to the mystery of your servanthood." As we raise our faces from the altar of Jesus's own obedience we face our own infidelities, our own deafness to the voice of the Father who always calls us in His Son to listen, to listen to His voice of truth, of goodness. God is enjoining us, "Do not turn your face from Me, do not cover the ears of your heart by a subtle movement of the will. No, kiss the truth I bring to you. Receive the truth that you know dwells in your conscience by my own Spirit."

And so, the deacon then invokes the Spirit in the Penitential Rite. He calls out for the mercy of God. After the kiss he leads the congregation to confess sin, a prayer that brings to mind the reality of the choice to sin, the choice to weaken the communion we are to have with the self-giving Christ. Sin is a choice always for the self, always in defense of our unpurified desires. *Sin is always in the service of hiding from the truth and beauty of divine love*. It is a choice to be led by fear. It is the deepest of all fears, *the fear of trusting God* with our freedom. And so in fear we turn back upon *our own wounded* resources.

Deacon, you have kissed both the altar in reverence and the face of Christ in betrayal. Such is our human condition, one that ought not surprise or depress us, but one that we ought to all fight against. Sin's hold over our affections is real, and so is our history of hiding in sin when we become stressed, anxious, fearful, lonely; when we have, in other words, refused to kiss the face of truth. Such a kiss can only mean transformation, conversion and change.

Such a kiss we are not ready for, so we continue to kiss the face of Christ in Judas-like fashion, using a sign of intimacy in an inverted and pathological way. At times, we live only in the *appearance* of communion, but in reality choose to remain deeply attached to our own cramped and self-centered choices.

Let us spend a few minutes with this prayer of conversion, slowly speaking its truth and attending to the movements of our hearts as we do so. Let us listen to this prayer, the Confiteor, *as our own....*

I confess to almighty God,
and to you, my brothers and sisters,
that I have sinned through my own fault,
in my thoughts and in my words,
in what I have done, and in what I have failed to do;
and I ask blessed Mary, ever virgin,
all the angels and saints,
and you, my brothers and sisters,
to pray for me to the Lord our God.[4]

As one of the ordinary custodians of the Penitential Rite at Mass how do we think about our own entry into the mys-

---

4. When Form A of the Penitential Rite is used, the deacon must learn from the presider before Mass begins whether the deacon or the presider will lead the assembly in the recitation of the Confiteor. The rubrics imply that Form B of the Penitential Rite is reserved to the presider. In Form C, it is preferred that the deacon announces the invocations; however, the presider or another minister (e.g., the cantor) may do so.

tery of confessing sin? The deacon invites entry into the mystery of confessing sin, the mystery of living in the light, of not hiding, of not calling the darkness light. Liturgically there might be many reasons for the deacon to be so entrusted, some theological, some simply pragmatic, but what does such a duty mean to our *own* diaconal identity? Further, in what ways do we *continue* to face the truth about our need for forgiveness and mercy beyond the altar? In what ways do we continue to encourage the laity to metaphorically kiss the altar of sacrifice as they proceed deeper and deeper into their own mind-boggling mission to transform culture in the light of Christ's mysteries?

Take some time and silently receive what the Spirit is teaching you about your own sinful leanings and about your call to pray with others about overcoming sin.

St. Francis de Sales once noted that "we must not be disturbed at our sins, since for us *perfection consists in fighting against them.*"[5] In our diaconal ministry we are always aware of the creative tension that calls to us, to fight against the temptations we ourselves fall under while simultaneously speaking words of hope and conversion to the people our ministry leads us to assist. As men who face the truth by kissing the mystery of Christ's own death upon the altar, we want to become lovers of truth and not simply its chanters. We come to love truth by suffering its arrival in our hearts. As our affection for sin is healed over many years of receiv-

5. *Introduction to the Devout Life*, The First Part, Sec. 5 (New York: Image), 47–49.

ing the sacrament of penance, assisting at Mass, praying the Liturgy of the Hours, and receiving the truth spoken to us by our wives, coworkers and families, we know that normally receiving such truth can be painful. With grace, however, we can come to welcome the truth about ourselves because we know that it is a bracing gift from God. We embrace the truth because we want to place no obstacle between His love for us and our need for His salvation. The choosing of sin should not surprise us; we are wounded, broken and bent toward the ego from the moment of our birth. It has and always will be easier for the human to choose the self than to choose what is good since that facility in choosing immorality is the core of the spiritual wound. This ease with which we choose sin changes, however, when we pray to have God's mercy enter us right at the site of our wounds, to have Him enter our hearts with grace *in and through our very desire to sin*. He must enter there because that is the opening, the wound He must heal. Physicians don't heal a broken bone or pulled muscle in the leg by working on the shoulder: no, *they work at the site of the wound*. Let the divine physician heal us by yielding up to Him our greed, pride, lust, sloth, anger, gluttony and envy. "Lord, touch me at the site of my wound." We have to be very particular about the wound needing divine attention; God doesn't heal vaguely; He heals exactly. He heals root and stem. "'What do you want me to do for you?' He said, 'Lord, let me see again'" (Luke 18:41). Not only will Christ heal our sins but in so doing He will also establish

His reign in our hearts more deeply. "He must increase, but I must decrease" (John 3:30).

During the Penitential Rite at Mass we ask the Lord to heal not only our venial *sins* but the *affection* that we hold for all our sins. It is our routine affection for sin that keeps us enslaved. Christ has to enter the wounds of our soul to heal not simply our actions but the REASONS why we choose sin over and over again. *Why* do I derive pleasure or some consolation from greed, lust, anger? This spiritually pathological pleasure is what needs to be healed by Christ. Once our affection for sin is deflated we can then taste the newness of freedom.

So from the altar where we assist prayerfully, we take the mysteries to the secular world. Carrying the life, death and resurrection within us by faith we do our best to listen to those in the workplace and beyond testify to their own need for healing. We listen to them from within hearts configured by ordination to Christ's own servant heart. We are listening not as psychologists or troubleshooters but as public ministers of the gospel ordained to bear the mystery of Christ's own eager availability to the world. We can, therefore, speak few but potent words of hope and healing into the wounds of the laity. God has placed us within the secular world for that very reason…to mediate in prayer, word and action the healing presence of Christ, the desire of God to enter the hiding places that keep us from His mercy. "But the Lord God called to the man, and said to him, 'Where are you?' He said, 'I heard the sound of you in the garden, and I was afraid, because I was naked; and I hid myself" (Gen 3:9–10). The deacon stands ready to hear these words uttered in the ordinary stream of life and to gently point those who speak them, or infer them, back to the extraordinary stream of healing that is the Eucharist, and the sacrament of penance.

Recall a time in your ministry when you were unexpectedly given the opportunity to heal another Christian with your words or behavior. Sit with this memory in prayer for a few minutes and receive again the graces that Christ wants to continue to give you from that choice of yours to be eagerly available to the spiritual needs of another.

As the *National Directory for the Formation of Permanent Deacons* urges, "To live their ministry to the fullest deacons must know Christ intimately so that He may shoulder the burdens of their ministry" (n. 62). Assisting at the altar and giving witness to the mystery of the Eucharist with our service is the fullness of living our ministry. To live our ministry is to first and foremost withhold *nothing* from Christ, who approaches only to bestow mercy and the gift of the fullness of our vocation. At times we are afraid Christ will take something from us and so we withdraw from His light. What does Christ take? *Only our sins.* If we give them to Him at the Eucharist we will know the intimacy He wishes to gift us with. This intimacy is experienced not as fleeting emotion but as communion, a communion that is anchored in the act of our receiving love and forgiveness. This receptivity, then, becomes our way of *being*; hence this communion with Christ is our way of *living*. The full fruit of this interiority is tasted not necessarily by ourselves but by the people we minister to. Normally we bestow the healing of Christ upon people according to the level that we have received it ourselves. The lives of the saints give testimony to this sacred exchange.

Some deacons recoil from such intimacy with Christ and retreat to a more comfortable ministry of "helping out." Here, in the safety of doing good deeds, I can know the affirmation of a job well done. No one needed ordination to live such a life. *To miss intimacy with Christ is to miss one's ordination*; it is to have never fully received the gift and power. As deacons we did not receive a catechist certificate enabling us to perform a competency, we received the Spirit of Christ the Servant; Christ the one who came not to be served but to serve. In order to have the potency of ordination released one has to receive this Spirit as the energy of your ministry. "Come Holy Spirit and take me, possess me so that I can descend from the *sanctuary of service* so as to enter ordinary life and preside at *the liturgy of charity* in the power of our love for one another." At this level of presence to God and His people your ministry WILL HEAL.

Spend some time with Christ meditating upon His will that you serve the people as healer.

Christ, how close do you really want to come to me? How deeply do you really want to enter my soul? I do want what You want, so please help me to receive You at new levels of love. In so doing, release the power of healing in my service; release your Spirit in my attention to your people.

From out of the mystery of your being forgiven by Christ, and your subsequent contemplation of such an unmerited gift, humility will be given to you. We don't set out to become humble; we find ourselves humiliated and from being brought low we are ushered into living a life of truth. In this life we possess a real sense of our self-worth, an authentic grasp of our gifts and talents. To live in this way is another dimension of freedom that Christ wants to bestow. From this humility you will speak the truth to sinners, and sinners will seek out conversion. Some deacons who have entered orders after much secular success struggle mightily with allowing Christ to gift them with His humility. They never fully let Christ into their wounds, because it wasn't their wounds that led them to ordination, it was their secular competency and success. The formators of such deacons were also dazzled by this man's native talents and confused secular competency for ministerial fidelity. Once ordained, this man has struggles entering the Confiteor, and so can be somewhat rejected by the people he serves because the *light is shining on him and not from within him*. Such a man is confused by his isolation in ministry as the people leave him and go looking for Christ elsewhere. Meanwhile, he remains in ministry simply serving up professional skills that are sufficient but not complete.

Ironically, something similar occurs with the self-identified simple candidate for ordination as well. "Oh I am just a simple laborer, bureaucrat or maintenance man," he says. This identification can then become a cover for him to hide behind. Christ is calling him to suffer a new growth in intellect or in personal communication skills but such human development frightens this man. He uses spiritual terms, pious terms and virtuous terms to deflect the truth that he needs to embrace. He doesn't find theology useful; he doesn't want to learn much; he just wants to pray with the people, and visit the sick and imprisoned. His humble disposition makes a nice picture, but then after ordination he grabs the pulpit or the classroom lectern. In the pulpit his lack of intellectual curiosity and *acedia* infects the people with boredom and even doubt over the compelling nature of the gospel. His humility corrupts the very people he wanted to piously and simply serve. He wants to appear like a finished humble product but since he refused to enter into the Penitential Rite, its purifying effects remain elusive.

Another type of dysfunctional deacon uses affective charm to woo the people he serves into liking him. Part of his ministry is to receive the affirmation of the crowd. He possesses many natural gifts and talents; he also has a level of talent that carries a certain pastoral usefulness, but at home with his wife this deacon stumbles. He acts unjustly toward his wife and family and makes them labor under his own inability to enter an authentic interior conversion which carries urgent self-knowledge. He lacks the courage to name his own sins and spends his energy not being tutored by the truth but avoiding it, so humility cannot be received. His wife loves him and so indicates this incongruence between his domestic life and his ministry. He does not receive this message with openness, thus limiting the depth to which he can enter the Penitential Rite he initiates at the Eucharist.

Spend some time in prayer meditating on any residual healing you may need that you did not receive in your diaconal formation. Ask Christ to bring to the light those areas of your heart that you have refused to show Him during formation, those areas that you were perhaps ashamed of or embarrassed by…let Him heal you now.

"Jesus, show me where I need to be purified of my own unwillingness to receive your truth and love. Where are my blind spots to living a deeper, fuller ongoing formation and conversion? Help me to receive your truth about my soul from any and all messengers you send my way. These 'angels' carry my own liberation; may I receive them with gratitude and not resent their being sent to me."

Meditation Three
Proclaiming the Gospel

"Receive the Gospel of Christ, whose herald you now are.
Believe what you read, teach what you believe, and practice what you teach."

Ordination Rite of the Deacon

Here, in the prayer uttered at diaconal ordination, is the very heart of diaconal identity. It invites the candidate into a profound receptivity to the word (listening) along with the consequent competencies to discern and teach the truth. Such a love of and formation by the word leads the deacon to enflesh in service what has fully engaged his mind and heart in contemplation.

We cannot simply approach this call to receive the word in a functional way, looking upon it simply as a set of duties one performs to proclaim the gospel in the midst of the Eucharistic liturgy. The call to be a herald runs deeper and finds it fulfillment in loving the word, and inviting the living word to become internalized in our hearts. The word has to define the deacon. We, like Paul, must preach. We cannot contain it: "If I proclaim the gospel, this gives me no ground for boasting, for an obligation is laid on me, and woe betide me if I do not proclaim the gospel!" (1 Cor 9:16). This preaching may occur within our pastoral assignments or it may be more prevalent in our witness given at our secular profession. No matter, the word has to become established in us for our diaconal vocation to be fully received. To love the word and internalize it in our hearts is not simply confined to our commitment to read and pray the scripture in private prayer, or enter deeply into the Liturgy of the Hours. Rather, such internalization is God's work, a work that is completed when His grace meets our desire. Do you desire to think out of the word of God, to make decisions based upon its wisdom and principles? This is, of course, a simple question with a simple answer for the deacon, "Yes, of course." Desire, however, is measured by its finding rest in its goal. Desire is not wishing; it is executing behaviors that are initiated by our holy affections. To have holy affections we have to pray that our desires will be purified and our will strengthened by sharing in Christ's own obedience: His own rapt listening to the Father.

In order to internalize the word as our inner compass we need to suffer the coming of Christ's own love of the Father's will. This can seem daunting, but Christ will gift us with it, *if* we ask. You will know when you have received this gift when your desire to read and contemplate the word becomes your food. Such food is consumed out of necessity and not simply taste. When Christ shares His spirit of obedience with us we will need to listen to the truth, behold the truth in our hearts spiritually through contemplation, and speak only the truth from a pure conscience. This need to be obedient is not an external compulsion or a neurotic sense of being driven. This need to listen, to be obedient to the Father, exists within our hearts as peace, as fulfillment and the appropriation of our true identity. Albeit this peace is won at a price: the reconfiguring of our minds and hearts away from the values of this passing age and toward the truth of the word of God. This previous history of formation has to be purified. Such purification may induce suffering because of undue love of what assuages the ego. Grace as a herald purifies the ego; it cannot mollify it.

Christ has called deacons to communion with His own spirit of listening because He desires to disseminate His grace throughout the church and world by way of the ministry of the word. As one of His heralds, the deacon has an interior life that burns with a steady flame of light that guides him ever deeper into communion with Christ by a diaconal conscience formed and molded by rapt attention to the mystery of self-emptying love. This mystery *is that aspect of the word* that rivets the deacon's attention vocationally. If Christ's own self-donation is fully received *as the personal core of a deacon's public ministry* it will constitute his way of sanctification. Ideally, the deacon's reception of the book of gospels at his ordination ignites this life and ministry of humble self-donation.

Let's take a few minutes and receive the above meditation in prayer, listening particularly to those aspects of it that you naturally resist, and secondly, to those aspects that your heart desires more than ever. Offer the resistance up to Christ at the next Eucharist you assist at so He can soften any hardness of heart around needed conversion. Embrace the second aspect as the desire that Christ wants to give you at deeper and deeper levels.

Can you cry out to Christ for a share in His Spirit of obedience? What fears arise in you when you do? Do you want the word to become internalized within your heart so as to teach you from within? Are you open to having the word bear to your conscience the teaching of the Spirit and not the spirit of this age? What can you do so that you do not simply wish for this change but see that it becomes a central aspect of the ***desire*** *which is your prayer?*

The Prophetic Word

St. Paul taught, "Pursue love and strive for the spiritual gifts, and especially that you may prophesy" (1 Cor 14:1). In the context of our meditation on the word this is a most relevant challenge to deacons today. We are to pursue the love of God, the love of prayer, but this communion with Christ is at the service of our publicly identifying where God's word and work are being challenged. The church is waiting for us to prophesy. It is waiting for us to name where the word of God is being dismissed, undermined and rejected in our culture. We are called to name the false teachings which are put in the place of the truth of doctrine. Such prophecy is the strength that builds up the church (1 Cor 14:4). Communion with Christ in scriptural prayer is the way for the deacon to both receive grace and discern how best to articulate where grace is thwarted in contemporary society. To prophesy is not to speak one's own ideologies or to favor any political party platform. These types of homilies and lectures carry no power from God but simply secure our own biases and prejudices. To prophesy the deacon has to be purified by the word as it is manifest in church doctrine. Today, simply preaching the doctrine of the church on issues of economics, war, sex, marriage and family, abortion, end-of-life decisions, capital punishment, poverty, hunger or care for the environment is to shed light on where God's truth has been undermined and rejected. There are, of course, other issues that need to be discerned in the immediacy of each preacher's circumstance, those that cry out to be addressed locally. The doctrine of the church, however, stands as universal prophetic teaching, doctrine that all deacons ought to preach. In receiving the truth of doctrine and discerning how to prudently convey it, the deacon remains faithful to the priorities Paul desired to honor: prayerfully beg for the spiritual gift of prophecy.

Let us consider:

Are there moral and doctrinal issues that I will not discuss while preaching or teaching? Why is that? In refusing to preach on certain issues am I following fear or prudence, do I know how to distinguish between rationalization and prudent delay? Are there any teachings of the church that I privately dissent from? Have I discussed this with my spiritual director? Do I dissent from church teaching in public forums like preaching, teaching or counseling? Whose word do I herald: the church's, the spirit of this age, or my own?

If I only preach, teach or counsel what has been received by the church as doctrine, do I do so with compassion and understanding? Do I encourage people to enter these truths under the guidance of prayer and spiritual direction or do I present them in legalistic or authoritarian ways? Do I see the beauty and power of the truth to invite people to endure its entry into their hearts or do I wish to impose my timetable upon grace and conversion? Do I preach doctrine out of fear or anger? Were you wounded by some of the experimental catechetical and clerical formation of the past decades and now wish to set things straight?

God, I love your word. Help me to be faithful, to reject dissent and to embrace your teaching with joy. Help me also to teach the faith with patience, compassion and ultimate trust in your salvific and universal will. I affirm that your grace has the power to convert hearts and that I assist in that power by faithfully proclaiming what was entrusted to me at my ordination: the teachings of the Catholic Church.

Formation in the Word

If scripture becomes our touchstone for intimacy with God then assuredly our minds will be brought beyond what currently engages them. The Spirit who dwells within our hearts and minds will tutor us in the ways of holiness *if* we commit ourselves to know divine revelation in the context of the church. What we are looking for as deacons is to come to possess and be possessed by the same mind that led Christ to a ministry of eager availability. Devotion to the word, as our touchstone for prayer, can help purify our desires as we enter the diaconate more fully, thus establishing within us a will and mind to embrace such Christlike availability. Calling down the Spirit of Christ as we pray through and study the scriptures defines the proper disposition of the deacon as he engages the texts. With such devotion it will not be long before the Spirit moves the pool of the heart as He did at the pool of Bethesda (John 5:1ff). From such healing the scriptures will become more and more the locus of divine encounter for the deacon. By way of this encounter the deacon's love for the scriptures will grow. From within this personal love of the word of God he will come to know it as the purest place for him to receive a mind beyond the one he now possesses (*metanoia*). Such a love of scripture will form his mind to be one that *seeks after only the promptings of the Spirit* (cf. 1 Cor 2:13).

Once scripture is established in the heart as one of the privileged places for meeting God, deacons will expectantly approach contemplative reading in order to receive a portion of Christ's own eager availability. All deacons should long to enter in faith the words of St. Paul, "[we are] servants of Christ and stewards of God's mysteries" (1 Cor 4:1). The deeper the word of God forms the conscience of the deacon, the more he will be able to be that steward of the mysteries within the secular world of his work, recreation and civic duty. To be a steward of the mysteries is to guard the place where God lives. The deacon then acts in a role of hospitality, opening the door to the mysteries, introducing them to others, and protecting their power and dignity by being faithful to their true meaning. To be formed in eager availability then is to be simultaneously formed to welcome the place where God lives (the sacraments) into your heart and to usher others into that same place as well.

Within scripture we find several key examples of how Christ himself ushered others into the mystery of His presence, and was eagerly available to deepen His own communion with the Father's love.

First, **Christ was eagerly available to the Father**. This openness to listen raptly to the Father is the hallmark of Christ's own human nature. He decided freely to go where the Father called Him, to speak what the Father shared with Him and dwell where the Father dwelled as evidenced by Christ seeking out time for prayer. Let us prayerfully receive this great mystery of Jesus into our own consciences and hearts by attending to how such communion with the Father was expressed in the Gospel of John.

a. John 5:17–30. "Very truly, I tell you, the Son can do nothing on his own, but only what he sees the Father doing; for whatever the Father does, the Son does likewise. The Father loves the Son and shows him all that he himself is doing....For just as the Father has life in himself, so he has granted the Son also to have life in himself...my judgment is just, because I seek to do not my own will but the will of him who sent me."
b. John 7:25–30. "Now some of the people of Jerusalem were saying, 'Is not this the man whom they are trying to kill? And here he is, speaking openly....Can it be that the authorities really know that this is the Messiah? Yet we know where this man is from; but when the Messiah comes, no one will know where he is from.' Then Jesus cried out as he was teaching in the temple, 'You know me, and you know where I am from. I have not come on my own. But the one who sent me is true, and you do not know him. I know him, because I am from him, and he sent me.' Then they tried to arrest him, but no one laid hands on him, because his hour had not yet come."
c. John 8: 28. "So Jesus said, 'When you have lifted up the Son of Man, then you will realize that I am he, and that I do nothing on my own, but I speak these things as the Father instructed me.'"

Do I wish to share in such profound communion with Christ's own obedience to His Father? This sharing in His own rapt listening to the Father is what he wants to give to His deacons so that they can be stewards of the mysteries, caring not for what is theirs but for what has been entrusted to them by God.

Second, **Christ was available to take people beyond where they were to where they are meant to be**—do you take people into true worship? Do you give living water?

Take some time to prayerfully read the story in John of the woman at the well. It begins:

> Jesus said to her, "Give me a drink." (His disciples had gone to the city to buy food.) The Samaritan woman said to him, "How is it that you, a Jew, ask a drink of me, a woman of Samaria?" (Jews do not share things in common with Samaritans.) Jesus answered her, "If you knew the gift of God, and who it is that is saying to you, 'Give me a drink,' you would have asked him, and he would have given you living water....Everyone who drinks of this water will be thirsty again, but those who drink of the water that I will give them will never be thirsty. The water that I will give will become in them a spring of water gushing up to eternal life." The woman said to him, "Sir, give me this water, so that I may never be thirsty or have to keep coming here to draw water"....The woman said to him, "I know that Messiah is coming"

> (who is called Christ). "When he comes, he will proclaim all things to us." Jesus said to her, "I am he, the one who is speaking to you"....Then the woman left her water jar and went back to the city. She said to the people, "Come and see a man who told me everything I have ever done! He cannot be the Messiah, can he?" They left the city and were on their way to him.... Many Samaritans from that city believed in him because of the woman's testimony, "He told me everything I have ever done." So when the Samaritans came to him, they asked him to stay with them; and he stayed there for two days. And many more believed because of his word. They said to the woman, "It is no longer because of what you said that we believe, for we have heard for ourselves, and we know that this is truly the Savior of the world."
>
> John 4:7–42

Note how Christ progressively moves the woman into a deeper trust of himself as a person. He invites her to listen to Him through her own desires: thirst, the longing to be loved by a husband, and worship, the desire to find the true God. He then speaks to these desires and gives them a correct orientation so that they may be fulfilled. She recognizes that Christ bears not simply answers *but a way to find meaning* and the way to purify and order human desires. This way is entered by way of surrender, by way of yielding to the Father who seeks out his people. We, too, bring others to this same point by giving witness to Christ and pointing to him as the fulfillment of all human desire and longing.

Do you listen intently not only to what people say but to the longings that motivate what they say? Can you help people relate their desires with what rivets the church's imagination and desire: the paschal mystery?

Notice that after the woman receives the healing/prophetic message from Christ she leaves her former ways of satisfying desire ("she left her water jar and went into town") and endeavors to spread the word about the encounter she had with Christ. Our goal in receiving the depths of scripture in our own prayerful encounter with Christ is to be able to encourage others to leave their former ways of deriving spiritual nourishment and refreshment and take up a new way: the way of receiving living water. Our evangelical desire motivates us to introduce people to the possibility of having our desires satiated. We long to have the people we serve never thirst again since we know that Christ is the water sought and found.

Do we make ourselves available to people at this level of vulnerability, at the level where our conversation with them IN CHRIST may lead them beyond the mind they now possesses to come to a new mind? Of course our mission is to leave them to rest in Christ, not ourselves, and to find their fulfillment only in Christ. Our eager availability to listen to their deepest desires only serves this encounter and it is our delight to hear people say, "We no longer believe because of your word; for we have heard for ourselves, and we know that this is truly the savior of the world."

Prayerfully enter the scripture above and ask the Lord to tutor you in how to listen to the desires of the people you serve so that you may speak a word of hope, liberation or orientation into those desires. "Lord, may I listen to others with your Spirit and therefore derive the wisdom I need to successfully hear, name and instruct the desires of the people you send to me for healing, teaching and service."

Third, **Jesus was available to the secular realities of His time**.

The deacon's eager availability within secular realities can be likened to the parable of the great feast (Luke 14:15ff). In this story a servant is told to go to the poor, and fill the house of the Lord with people who will feast on His banquet. This servant embodies an invitation from God, "if the people will not come to me and receive the grace of communion at worship then I will go in search of them and 'compel' them to come." The compulsion in this case, however, is not a physical urging, but a compulsion by way of beauty. United with the One in whose name he searches for the poor, the deacon can open the hearts of those who witness the beauty of his Christlike love attending to human need. Witnessing the beauty of seeing pastoral love in the secular world carries with it a call to the banquet of the Eucharist, a selfless love that carries intimations of the incarnation. There is a *diakonia* of the whole church. All who receive the mystery in Holy Communion are summoned to "go in Peace to love and serve the Lord," but the deacon publicly stands for the church in his comings and goings in the nooks and crannies of secular culture. It is this *public identity* born of his *call from Christ and confirmed by the bishop* that makes his radical availability to the mystery and to the spiritual desires of the people effective and iconic.[6] In Luke the master of the house keeps asking the servant to go out again and again until his house is filled. He also keeps asking the deacon to go deeper and deeper in the world to find those whom the Lord wishes to love within the banquet of his eternal self-donation. Thus the deacon here is seen to be one embedded in the secular world and not simply an employee of the church. To be a deacon is to cherish one's own link to the secular/lay life as well to cherish one's ordained link to the mysteries of the altar, relaxing this tension for no one, but finding within this Spirit-supported tension one's very own mission, one's very contribution to the ministry of the church.

Spend some time praying with those themes in this chapter that challenged you the most. What themes did you embrace in joy, which ones might you have resisted as it intimated a needed conversion?

6. In other writings I have referred to this availability as being the *presider at that liturgy of charity*. See my "Presiding at the Liturgy of Charity: The Deacon's Spiritual Identity," *Studies in Spirituality* 17 (2007): 185–96.

Meditation Four
The Prayer of the Faithful

To evangelize is not only to preach the Gospel but also to listen to the response given by the people to such preaching. By listening to this response the content for the next part of the Liturgy of the Word can emerge, the Prayer of the Faithful (the General Intercessions). When the truth of God's love goes forth from the pulpit in counsel or in the adult faith formation process there can be joy or sorrow, sometimes both! One can receive the word joyously knowing that to receive it will completely change one's life. Thus sorrow or fear can mix with joy and hope. From within this complexity may arise the need to seek counsel or prayer from priests and deacons. When this request for counsel is responded to by the deacon, he seeks to listen to the sufferings and hopes of the person before him. Out of this prayerful listening he notes the crosses carried by his neighbors and seeks to help them place these crosses within the paschal mystery of Christ as it envelops us in the celebration of the Eucharist.

To pray the Prayer of the Faithful with the congregation is to seek to voice their deepest desires, deepest wounds and deepest hopes. In some cases these desires will be familiar and routine. For example we always pray for the church, our enemies, and the sick and the dying. And yet, more novel and particular prayers will arise from the listening done by deacons during the normal course of their ministry. Not all prayers arise from people in their pain. Knowledge of what kind of prayer is needed also arises when a deacon contemplates the everyday actions he encounters at his place of employment or when relaxing in the neighborhood, or receiving the news online or on TV. Our intercessory prayers to God encompass both the need *to ask for relief of suffering* and *the thanksgiving offered for the many graces we behold each day*. We should ask for the gift of contemplative seeing. We should ask God to help our eyes connect to our love-imbued consciences. We don't just want to *look*, we want to *behold* in love. We want to have human activity in all its variations catch our eyes so that what we see stirs the affections of our heart and carries those truth-filled affections to our mind. Once we receive these activities within us fully, the deacon can then compose prayers of compassion, empathy, insight and gratitude.

In this act of beholding human activity we can rest with Christ in prayer and perhaps weep with him over Jerusalem or rejoice with him over revealing to the little ones what he has not revealed to the clever and wise (Matt 11:25). Ultimately we want to write or edit the Prayer of the Faithful in a way that connects human need and gratitude with a deep faith in the always-present love and providence of God. The deacon is called to attend to the needs of people in a spiritual way that incarnates itself concretely in charity.

> The saints...constantly renewed their capacity for love of neighbor from their encounter with the Eucharistic Lord, and conversely this encounter acquired its realism and depth in their service to others. Love of God and love of neighbor are thus inseparable, they form a single commandment. But both live from the love of God who has loved us first. No longer is it a question, then, of a "commandment" imposed from without and calling for the impossible, but rather of a freely-bestowed experience of love from within, a love which by its very nature must then be shared with others. Love grows through love. Love is "divine" because it comes from God and unites us to God; through this unifying process it makes us a "we" which transcends our divisions and makes us one, until in the end God is "all in all" (1 Cor 15:28).[7]

The Prayer of the Faithful, therefore, emerges from the spiritual eyes within the heart of the deacon. He sees differently than those who simply carry the burdens of the day or seek to unfold their plans for each day. These members of society are tempted to make the world small and

7. Benedict XVI, *Deus Caritas Est* (2005), n. 18.

without transcendent meaning. The deacon, as sacred minister, carries within him the hope that grace will give him and others new eyes with which to see. These new eyes survey the *depths* of meaning found in the everyday, they do not *simply notice* what is before them. The deacon who contemplates the world sees with the eyes of Christ. This holy sight is purified and received in a life made vulnerable to the word in holy reading, and in a life spent open to the mystery of Christ's self-donation as He lived it and deems to share it in the Eucharist. To pray the deepest needs of the people is to receive these needs and these people from within the deepest point of communion with Eucharistic self-giving. If the Prayer of the Faithful springs from such depths, then it will be fruitful and not simply perfunctory. Being one of the ministers who can intone the Prayer of the Faithful at the Eucharist, do you embrace its call to attend to the needs of the people to whom you have been given by Christ?

Have you asked for new eyes from Christ? "'What do you want me to do for you?' The blind man said to him, 'My teacher, let me see again.'" (Mark 10:51). As a deacon you want to see the poor in all their variety and complexity. The deacon is trained by his service at the altar to eagerly attend to those whom Christ came to save. This mystery of salvation is the mystery in which the deacon walks when assisting at the altar. Thus he is trained by prayer to attend to those persons eagerly searching to rest their burdened lives upon the cross of Christ. Are you aware of being tutored in the mysteries of Christ's self-offering to the poor while praying your service at the altar?

To pray in a petitionary manner is to be claimed by hope. To pray in such a way is to yield the ground of our purely secular interests to the interest of the Divine. It is God who is interested in those who suffer; we are mostly interested in our own welfare due to the wound of original sin. To pray this prayer of intercession is to regularly enter hope, a hope that stands against the prevailing culture limiting human meaning only to good times and economic well-being. This hope speaks a word to those who suffer—"even in your grief you are in communion with Christ, deep communion."

> In prayer we must learn what we can truly ask of God—what is worthy of God. We must learn that we cannot pray against others. We must learn that we cannot ask for the superficial and comfortable things that we desire at this moment—that meager, misplaced hope that leads us away from God. We must learn to purify our desires and our hopes. We must free ourselves from the hidden lies with which we deceive ourselves. God sees through them, and when we come before God, we too are forced to recognize them.[8]

The Prayer of the Faithful is an entry into those realities that have been discerned to be worthy of being asked of

8. Pope Benedict XVI, *Spes Salvi* (2007), n. 33.

God. First among these is holiness. It is the call to holiness that the church places at the heart of its life. On the day of our baptism we enter the drama of becoming saints; this grace is bestowed anew at our ordinations and configures us in a distinctive way to the servant mysteries of Christ. We are called to lead others into this mystery of holiness by the example of our lives. Therefore we should be leaders in teaching people how to pray for what is truly essential, what is truly in the heart of God to be given to His people—a share in the paschal mystery of Christ, a share in the holiness of God himself. High above all other desires this desire should always order our prayers of petition.

Second, we should ask God for the strength and the grace to live out our vocations faithfully. All too often Catholics think that fidelity to their particular calling is dependent upon their own wills and energies. To be faithful is this age we need to receive interior strength from the Spirit. We should ask God for the capacity to receive this strength regularly; otherwise we are building our lives upon sand (Matt 7:26).

Third, we ought to include prayers for the welfare of others. Simon Weil (1909–1943) once said that it is God's job to think of us, while it is our job to think of others. The great paradox of the spiritual life is that in forgetting our own needs God orders all things to their rightful completion. We do not have to plan and scheme to be safe in life; God is carrying us to the place of holiness if only we sacrifice the ego to His loving will in obedience. *To sacrifice in this way is the origin of Christian joy*. Once we believe that God is providential, we can then take up the call to be His hands in time. The worry for ourselves is on His shoulders; we now are free to discern how best to care for the needs of others. In such freedom we cry out to God to move the hearts of our parishioners so that they too might relinquish the stress of self-concern in favor of a fascinating life based upon receiving the love of the Father in all things.

Fourth, we ought to intercede for those who are severely suffering because they are on the cusp of losing faith or truly entering the paschal mystery and becoming saints. Those in such dire straits urgently need our prayers. It is to such that we race in pastoral ministry doing our best to bring a word of hope and Christ's loving presence into intolerable and mysterious suffering. This kind of grave suffering needs our particular attention since it usually involves innocent suffering: the death of child, the death of a spouse, the loss of health, the loss of a career, chronic illness and so much more. Beyond the prayer of intercession during Mass we also bring the prayer of the community and Christ to those who so suffer.

As deacons we cannot bring the sacrament of the sick into these situations when warranted but we *do* bring the fruit of our own interior appropriation of the paschal mystery, especially how this mystery relates to our ministerial and familial experience. Our formation has given us some skills in being present to those in traumatic situations, but more vitally, we have taken the journey to holiness seriously so that Christ can be recognized in our presence.

What we suffer in our own vocations and prayer life ought not to viewed less seriously than what we might have learned in a pastoral counseling class. The two interpenetrate and inform one another.

Beyond these four suggestions there are many other needs appropriate to the Prayer of the Faithful. We receive this capacity to formulate prayers of petition with great humility and gratitude. It is one of our precious ministries as deacon. It signals the trust of the church in and because of our presence in the daily lives of the people of our diocese.

Have you ever composed your own Prayer of the Faithful for the celebration of Sunday Mass? Does being designated to recite or compose the Prayer of the Faithful enter your own spiritual life in a concrete way?[9]

9. "After the priest, the deacon, in virtue of the sacred ordination he has received, holds first place among those who minister in the Eucharistic celebration. For the sacred order of the diaconate has been held in high honor in the church even from the time of the apostles. At Mass the deacon has his own part in proclaiming the gospel, in preaching God's word from time to time, in announcing the intentions of the Prayer of the Faithful, in ministering to the priest, in preparing the altar and serving the celebration of the sacrifice, in distributing the Eucharist to the faithful, especially under the species of wine, and sometimes in giving directions regarding the people's gestures and posture." General Instruction of the Roman Missal (2002), chapter 3, n. 94.

Meditation Five

The Mystery of the Water and Wine

"By the mystery of this water and wine may we come to share in the divinity of Christ who humbled himself to share in our humanity."

from the *Roman Missal,*
"The Liturgy of the Eucharist":
The Preparation of the Altar and the Gifts

We move now from the Liturgy of the Word into the Liturgy of the Eucharist. As deacons we belong at the altar of service. Liturgically it is a very simple service we perform...it is a nonessential service. The priest *can* certainly celebrate the Eucharist without us being there and yet the service of Christ Himself is so great within this sacrament, total self-donation, that the church wishes to embody symbolically *the service* and *the sacrifice* of Christ together on the altar. This full symbol is analogous to the one promoted when both species—bread become body and wine become blood—are offered to the people at holy communion. The deacon's service, albeit humble, visually draws out one of the essential truths of the paschal mystery....His **sacrifice** (priestly identity of Christ) **was** a service (*diakonia*). Of course the whole Christ is the bread become His body, but for a fuller symbol the congregation also receives the wine become His blood. Around the altar deacons are like that fuller symbol wherein their physical presence serving at the altar highlights a deeper dimension of the mystery of Christ. He is THE DIVINE ONE who sacrifices as a service to others. The deacon as assistant and the priest as representative of Christ's sacrificial self-offering invite the members of the church during worship *to receive the grace of so great a love*. If it is received then they can give testimony as to how the divine elevates and inhabits the human for the healing and salvation of each person.

As the deacon moves toward the altar we are charged to prepare the place of offering, the place of the sacrificial meal. It is a simple service: providing linens, placing prayer books, arranging chalices and patens, filling cups with wine and water. We simply prepare for the sacrifice by our service. In so doing our minds and hearts are drawn to our pastoral ministry. We prepare the people for their many sacrifices too. By our service, our eager availability as spiritual leaders, we assist the laity to offer themselves as acceptable sacrifices to the Lord. This preparation is mostly accomplished in our *humble fellowship* with them as coworkers in the vineyard, as fellow married persons and parents, as employees at local businesses. But, again, we are not simply mute witnesses standing by others: we are spiritual leaders drawing out faith and drawing our people deeper into the interior mysteries of Christ. No believer ought to bear the sufferings and sacrifices of this age without being accompanied by and drawing meaning from the life, death and resurrection of Christ. Each of us will go to the cross with Christ, since as deacons we prepare the hearts of our people for this sacrifice by way of our service. So we serve the people of our diocese in order that they may more effectively receive the intimacy of Christ during their own self-offering to the Father, their own offering of body and blood, their own "yes" to all that is given within the ordinariness of their days. In performing such ordinary activities at the altar, God is preparing us not to spurn the grace hidden in everyday life. The dignity of our call is to assist the laity to do the same. We are to point to the realities that carry the mingling of this water (the ordinary) and wine (the sacred).

At the side of the altar we take the water, the water that flowed from the side of the temple, gushing forward, greening and healing all, and we pour a small drop into the wine that is to become blood. When we do this simple act we meditate upon the density of God's own generosity toward the world: "By the mystery of this water and wine may we come to share in the divinity of Christ, who humbled himself to share in our humanity." Here, in meditation, the sacred and profane are brought together in the mystery of the new temple that is Christ himself. Our own lives of water, humble ordinary service, flow to their proper end and are taken up into the complex beauty of the wine of divine self-giving. In this wine we taste our true potential as persons ordered toward transfiguration in Christ. As deacons we marvel at these words spoken only in our hearts, given to us, entrusted to us not as words of consecration but as words of inspiration to our own sacramental mystery—bringing the sacred to bear upon the ordinary sacrifices of our people.

The deacon imbeds himself in the secular world in order to evangelize it. He meditates deeply upon the mysteries of the altar, the salvation brought about by Christ's loving obedience, and seeks to have this same disposition guide him throughout the work week. The deacon mingles among the sacred and profane day in and day out in the vocation that is his and his alone, fruitfully bearing the tension within him of the lay-clerical life. His passion is to utter the words and enact behavior that readies others to receive the divine in the midst of the ordinary. This passion does *not* carry itself in an annoying and ultimately fruitless display of public preaching. Rather, the deacon carries the seeds of conversion by establishing fellowship and helping others in the public realm to form their consciences according to the wisdom received by their active love of the life, death and resurrection of Christ. The deacon endeavors to guide the minds of the laity and support them in both their knowledge of prudent discipleship and courageous witness.

This simple prayer at the side of the altar is truly our intercession before God. "Lord Jesus, please give me the wisdom to know how to invite the laity into the sacred, and to affirm the secular as capable of receiving the sacred."

Return in your imagination to a time when you mingled in the ordinary events of the day so as to bring others into an awareness of the divine. Where do you draw your most powerful support from in the work of raising others to a life of prayer?

Meditation Six

Elevating the Chalice

During the Eucharistic prayer we abide in the space with the priest at the altar, we linger in silence like Mary and St. John under the cross, prayerfully interceding for the intentions that have been pressed upon our hearts by the people of the diocese. Like Mary and John we carry the sorrows of many in our prayers, we have no answers, we simply offer the mysteries to the people when they cry in our presence or grieve over the loss of someone or something meaningful. We stand at the altar for them and with them plead with the saints for our people's liberation from sin, sickness, ignorance and poverty. At one point the very words of Christ are intoned and His mystery descends upon the altar to feed us, to give us life. Next, we are given the chalice by the priest to elevate with him as he elevates the body of Christ. Here, in this moment, the fullness of symbols are present: the total Christ in the sacrament and the total virtues of Christ, sacrifice and service, in the two ordained ministers, priest and deacon. As we hold the chalice the priest recites, "through Him, with Him, and in Him, in the unity of the Holy Spirit, all glory and honor is yours almighty Father, forever and ever." The people, and the deacon, respond, "Amen." Here the real presence of Christ as gift for all creation leads to a crescendo of adoration for the Father.

This doxology ("through Him, with Him...") gathers up our gratitude which is offered to God for the grace that comes in the mystery of Christ's life, death and resurrection. As deacons we stand amazed that we are given the privilege to embody with the priest the full symbol of Christ's own sacrifice. Gratitude is not only universal at this point but also is very personal for the deacon, "Jesus thank you for my call, thank you for inviting me right into the gift as it is sacramentally offered each Sunday. I want to be transformed by my participation in orders; this sacramental ordination given to me by way of this great sacrifice of yours."

Our prayerful presence at the altar during the doxology reminds us of the vital role praise and thanksgiving should play in the deeper reception of our vocation to the diaconate. It is only in and through Christ that we can be sustained in this call, a call that configures us to His service. In our faithfulness to the call to serve in Christ, God the Father does receive honor and glory. The Spirit breathes in us and moves our hearts to adore the one God who came and opened His own happiness to share it with us; a happiness defined as *diaconal* (Matt 20:28). It is the deacon's joy to give himself away in service. From this eager availability springs his own happiness—to thwart it is to refuse the joy Christ WANTS TO GIVE.

While the priest is reciting the Eucharistic prayer we are silently attending to the Christological mystery in our imagination. We are like Mary and John beneath the cross as they contemplated the wonder of Christ's *kenosis* (self-emptying) amidst, in and through their own grief. In the chapel of the Institute for Priestly Formation where I work, there is a fascinating depiction of the cross in iconic form wherein Mary is seen in tears on the left side of the cross and John is seen in a traditional pose of contemplation on the right side of the cross. This artwork depicts a paradoxical scene: we are led to the deepest of contemplation through grief. What are *we* grieving for, however? As deacons we are exposed to a great deal of messiness in the human condition. We have an ideal of what Catholic life should be like but we keep bumping up against sin, finitude, limit and ignorance. In truth, humans can be their own worst enemies. We see beauty, we desire it, but we are quite often incapable of receiving it and being molded by it. There is sadness at the heart of much human endeavor. At Golgotha Christ shared in this finitude and took on that which compounds it and confounds our desires to respond to true beauty—sin. Here at the Eucharist the mystery of Christ's great love for us is exposed: He even went into what we fear most—death, grief, sin, limit, ignorance, pain and sorrow. His love reached deep into these dark places, places that make us all cry with Mary. In our grief, however, we are led quietly by John into contemplation, to wonder over such a divine love. “Indeed, rarely will anyone die for a righteous person—though perhaps for a good person someone might actually dare to die. But God proves his love for us in that while we still were sinners Christ died for us” (Rom 5:7–8).

If our diaconal service is to be alive with spiritual energy we all must linger in this place of contemplative tears. In this place, at this altar, we are forged into mature men grown to full stature capable of integrating the sufferings of our own lives with the sufferings of our people’s, all in the context of receiving the mystery of Christ’s own self-offering—the holy way to cope with the human condition. Human grief is the sorrow we know in our sin. This sorrow wells up only if we are given the grace to let the mystery of Christ affect us. If we remain aloof and unavailable to His love upon the cross then we will never be broken, a brokenness that is essential to our being able to behold and desire a share in divine holiness.

As deacons we aspire to serve the church in Christ, and to do so we must carry with us the mystery of man. We need to possess the knowledge of conversion from sin, and the wounds of our own repentance from sin. These wounds are at first experienced as humiliation and embarrassment and perhaps unworthiness, but in grace these wounds become the birthplace of compassion and wisdom. “Therefore, I tell you, her sins, which were many, have been forgiven; hence she has shown great love. But the one to whom little is forgiven, loves little” (Luke 7:47). This doesn’t mean that those with few sins love only superficially, it means that those who do not know the depth of their sins, and therefore, the depth of the beauty of God's offer of forgiveness, love little. When the fullness of the truth of our sins is received by our consciousness we do not fall into guilt-ridden introspection, but are lifted up into and share in the grace of Christ's own charity.

As the deacon stands elevating the chalice, he stands at the heart of Calvary, at the core of the mystery of divine love. This love, poured out forever in the singular act of Christ upon the cross, awakens the deacon to depths of his own need for forgiveness, and the joy of his having received such here at the Mass and in the sacrament of penance. In this joy the deacon rushes toward the secular world with a service that originates in the liberating reality of "this is my body, which is given for you" (Luke 22:19).

Stay with the image of you lifting the chalice and in your imagination converse with Christ about your gratitude to Him over the forgiveness of sin.

Meditation Seven

Let Us Offer Each Other a Sign of Peace

What could be closer to man's deepest yearning than to possess peace in the depths of one's heart and peace between oneself and others, and more broadly, peace between nations. To be *in peace* is to be in a state of purified desire. No longer is one grasping to take power, influence to oneself, or create meaning for oneself. No longer is one stirred to anxious restlessness by living in and making choices consciously out of fear over what he or she lacks. Rather, in peace, one is thinking, desiring and choosing out of communion with the mystery of Christ's own love. Peace is being in communion with the divine mystery, receiving God at the very depths of vulnerability, from within a heart that stands open to intimacy and therefore suffering. For to receive the mystery of Christ is to live through the transformation of disordered desire and to know the pain of letting go what previously attracted you in order to take up a new attraction, conforming to the mystery of Christ.

And so, for deacons to invite others to offer peace to each other is an invitation ordered toward hope. We hope that the people we serve will be able to suffer the coming of peace in their own lives so as to center themselves not in some external identity grafted upon them by the consumer, entertainment and political culture. Rather, we hope to encourage our people to center themselves within the meaning of the self-donation of Christ to His bride, the church. This peace is the gift found within the very self-giving of Christ toward His bride *if* she receives it. We stand at the altar and invite the congregation to *acknowledge* the presence of the other person, the presence of another who is literally beyond one's immediate concerns and egocentric agendas, and so to begin a journey toward peace. In this journey the self is decentered in Christ and he leads the believer to the other, to the one who is beyond his or her control. In Christ we are tutored to entrust ourselves to the mystery of another person by extending ourselves not simply with a prayerful greeting but by way of a life of compassion. It is a simple gesture to shake the hand or embrace the person next to you in a pew, but this gesture contains the metaphor for all true peace: reaching out toward communion with another who is different, even as he or she remains *other*.

This celebration of difference, however, is not the maudlin diversity that is promoted by the political culture; rather this difference is one that stands to be tutored by truth and rests upon a will ordered toward the welfare of the other. Lacking these perspectives the culture can only promote a counterfeit peace: leaving the other alone to do as he or she pleases. There can only be true peace if love is conveyed by the promotion of the moral truth. In true peace there is union between different persons. In true peace there is no flattening of difference but instead difference is celebrated. The only reality eliminated in true peace is moral evil, thus leaving behind the freedom to love. How does one promote true peace as a deacon?

> Discovering that they are loved by God, people come to understand their own transcendent dignity, they learn not to be satisfied with only themselves but to encounter their neighbor in a network of relationships that are ever more authentically human. Men and women who are made "new" by the love of God are able to change the rules and the quality of relationships, transforming even social structures. They are people capable of bringing peace....Only love is capable of radically transforming the relationships that men maintain among themselves.[10]

This love is not the sentimental emotion that cynics reject whenever the word is mentioned by the church. It is, instead, the hard love that kept Christ pinned to the cross, and even more deeply kept His heart attuned to for-

---

10. Pontifical Council for Justice and Peace, *Compendium of Social Doctrine* (Washington D.C.: USCCB Publishing, 2005), n. 4.

giveness and compassion as he said "yes" to heal the suffering. From the Mass the deacon brings the message of this hard love to the culture in his relationships with the laity. The deacon first serves the nature of love among the persons he is sent to directly minister to, but he is attuned to the fact that these people have a whole network of relationships that can affect the transmission of the gospel and its fruit—peace—as well. The deacon doesn't *cause* peace, he *carries* it.

> Human relationships cannot be governed solely by the measure of justice: "The experience of the past and of our own time demonstrates that justice alone is not enough, that it can even lead to the negation and destruction of itself...justice must, so to speak, be 'corrected' to a considerable extent by that love which, as St. Paul proclaims, 'is patient and kind' or, in other words, possesses the characteristics of that merciful love which is so much of the essence of the Gospel and Christianity."[11]

For the deacon to carry the mercy mentioned above he must have first suffered its coming during and beyond his formal spiritual preparation for ministry. If this formation is accomplished he can better see who the leaders of the diocese might be in promoting the work of concretizing love within the social web. The deacon continually seeks to identify the lay leaders who will give witness to the pub-

11. Ibid, n. 206.

lic meaning of the gospel. Once found, the deacon offers all the resources at his disposal to deepen the formation of such leaders so that the mystery of Eucharistic love will not simply be known between individual persons but will come to full fruition as a social truth.

> No legislation, no system of rules or negotiation will ever succeed in persuading...peoples to live in unity, brotherhood and peace; no line of reasoning will ever be able to surpass the appeal of love. Only love, in its quality as "form of the virtues" [456], can animate and shape social interaction, moving it towards peace in the context of a world that is ever more complex. In order that all this may take place, however, it is necessary that care be taken to show love not only in its role of prompting individual deeds but also as a force capable of inspiring new ways of approaching the problems of today's world, of profoundly renewing structures, social organizations, legal systems from within. In this perspective love takes on the characteristic style of social and political charity.... Social and political charity is not exhausted in relationships between individuals but spreads into the network formed by these relationships, which is precisely the social and political community; it intervenes in this context seeking the greatest good for the community in its entirety....To love [an individual] on the social level means...to make use of social mediations to improve his [or her] life or to remove

> social factors that cause...indigence. It is undoubtedly...the work of mercy by which one responds here and now to a real and impelling need of one's neighbor, but it is equally [an] act of love to strive to organize and structure society so that one's neighbor will not find himself in poverty.[12]

It is clear from the Catholic Church's moral teachings that peace, the peace that is known in the Eucharist, will only take root in a culture if the network of human relations constructs a society of justice. As we deacons invite the congregation to share a sign of peace with one another during the Mass, we need to make it our constant intercessory prayer that within our ministry we may be able to form the persons who will carry that sign into the secular world.

Where in my ministry do I endeavor to embody a "ministry of reconciliation"? Where do I resist gaining prayerful competence in the social teachings of our church? Why?

What lay person most inspires you as a peacemaker? What were the formation factors in this life that made him or her an inspiration?

---

12. Ibid, n. 207–8.

Meditation Eight
The Mass Is Ended

As I was writing this book exciting news came from the Vatican that Pope Benedict XVI was contemplating changing the dismissal rite of the Mass from its present optional forms to new ones. Why is this exciting? If the dismissal rite comes to encompass any or all of the new suggested phrases the deacon would be more clearly articulating the beginning of the liturgy he presides over: *The mystery of the liturgy of charity*. The suggested phrases are:

Go and announce the Gospel of the Lord.
Go in peace, glorifying the Lord by your life.[13]

These new phrases more clearly capture the dynamic power of how Christ sends the laity into the fields of evangelical work. The mystery of the Eucharist is now full in their consciences, they are summoned to bear witness to

13. Catholic News Service, October 20, 2008; http://www.catholicnews.com/data/stories/cns/0805330.htm.

what they have just received and will continue to receive by their habit of prayer. The fruit of the Eucharist is the transformation of culture. In this transformation the laity gives witness to the power of Christ's presence influencing the judgment of their consciences. These judgments make up the public presence of the mystery of the church. In other words, the new optional phrases of the dismissal rite more clearly concentrate the mind of the laity around the dignity of *their* call. If they are not listening to the sending rite at the end of the Mass which the deacon intones, they will miss living out their own dignity because they will have missed how Christ has named them. As we intone the dismissal we are not passive bystanders in the mystery of public martyrdom since we are called by our vocation, unlike the priest, to follow the laity right out the doors of the church to stand by them in those same fields of evangelical courage.

If these changes to the liturgy occur, both the spiritual identity of deacons and the laity will have become more clearly articulated. We deacons, as noted above in Meditation Five, are coworkers in the vineyard with the laity by virtue of our being clerics who live a lay lifestyle. If we begin to intone these new phrases we will be intoning our own identity and encouraging the laity to take up theirs as well. The laity, in turn, will be receiving their identity, their mission, each time they assent to what they have received in the Eucharist, the very charism of Christ's own listening to the Father. If they have opened their hearts to receive this grace of obedience, then our intonation will be an occasion for them to claim this grace *in a determined way* as they disperse into the culture after Mass. Their interior listening to conscience, where Christ dwells, definitely marks them as ambassadors of the Eucharist.[14] But if the dismissal rite is not simply the end of the Eucharistic Liturgy but also the beginning of the liturgy of charity, what is this liturgy?[15]

The sacrament of orders keeps love alive in a sacramental way, assuring against its extinction. If *no others* were to love the poor, the deacon would keep the hope of such service alive. Within a spirituality of the diaconate, the very act of serving takes on a sacramental cast. In these acts that we perform grace is communicated in a characteristic way, in a way that establishes the hope that charity will never become extinct.

Our unique contribution to ecclesial ministry is to *preside at the liturgy of charity* in and through the grace of ordination and the sending by the bishop. Both the bishop and priest preside at the Eucharist, and from there they are called to charity. Alternately, deacons preside at the liturgy of charity, and from there we are called to assist at the mysteries of the Eucharist. It is not simply service or even charity that distinguishes our way to holiness, but a service and charity *contextualized in obedience to a bishop's commission*. Such a commission configures the deacon to Christ's public ministry of service.

---

14. John Paul II, *Dominicae Cenae*, "At the Eucharist Christ comes into the hearts of our brothers and sisters and visits their consciences." N. 6.

15. See Benedict XVI, *Deus Caritas Est*, esp. par. 22–23.

We deacons do not preside at the Eucharistic liturgy; rather, we intone, in its dismissal rite, the *initiation* of the *liturgy of charity*, charging all to "go in the peace of Christ to love and serve the Lord." This presidency is not a juridical one, but rather one of moral and spiritual collaboration with the mission of the laity. This collaboration is unique in that we, paradoxically, embody an *official ecclesial presence* within a *lay lifestyle*. From this unique vocation we are invited to animate the laity to public witness.

Unlike the priest, our words *do not* bring about the real presence of Christ in the Eucharist. In fact, the deacon utters *no words at all* in the liturgy he presides over, except in the silence of his heart as it communes with the mystery that has claimed his life: "[I] came not to be served but to serve" (Matt 20:28). At the dismissal rite, the Eucharist processes out of the church doors in the hearts of parishioners, not as an inert memory of a ritual that engaged only their time, but as a living call from Christ to go and transform culture. In so doing, the people extend the Eucharistic presence of Christ by way of their service and witness.

The altar and the needs of the many are integrated in the ministry of the bishop's envoy, that is, the deacon. We preside by distributing the *fruit* of the Mass—the divine life within us. This divine life, our spiritual life, first called us to orders and now inspires, directs, sustains and enables our outreach toward the needs of laity. Christian hope and charity find a home within official ecclesial ministerial structures by way of our witnessing to the virtue of self-donation born of the Eucharist, an action at the very core of the mystery of Christ. This service, of course, is spiritual, holy and not simply the result of natural virtue or the fruit of motivating ethics lectures we might have heard during formation classes. No, this service is our form of *in personae Christi*: Christ acting in us. We do not share in the priesthood. Since we share in orders, however, we receive a portion of the mystery of *Christ's own actions*. The priest shares in Christ's sacrificial self-offering in priestly thanksgiving—whereas we who are deacons receive that portion of Christ's own action which insures that the love of many will not grow cold (Matt 24:12).

Our presiding in charity within secular realities can be likened to the parable of the great feast (Luke 14:15ff) as noted above in Meditation Three. In this story the servant is told to go to the poor, and fill the house of the Lord with people who will feast at His banquet. In so going the deacon embodies an invitation from God, "if the people will not come to me and receive the grace of communion at the Banquet then I will go in search of them and 'compel' them to come." The compulsion in this case, however, is not a physical urging, but a compulsion *by way of beauty*. United with the One in whose name we search for the poor, we can, in our service, *break the hearts* of those who witness the beauty of love as it raptly attends to human need. The beauty of witnessing love in action calls people to the banquet of the Eucharist, selfless love carrying intimations of the incarnation. There is the *diakonia* of the whole church. We may carry this mystery of charity as the essence of our being in orders but we long to include *all members of the church* in such beauty.

In rendering our ministry, the deacon and those who assist him at *the altar of charity* create an icon for others to contemplate and behold. In this contemplative beholding during the liturgy of charity, we have something akin to Eucharistic adoration or the silence that enfolds the elevation of the Sacred Host during the Eucharistic Prayer. Those in the midst of secular concerns are drawn into the sight of others giving without concern for reward.

Most vitally, we welcome Christ's movements and stirrings within our own consciences. In so doing we are prompted to bear the power of the paschal mystery into the deepest cracks and crevices of popular and economic culture. Here, among the laity, as one who lives their life, we assist the laity to endure the word as it comes in truth. To endure the coming of the word affords us the strength to receive the truth and, once received, to witness to it. The sacramental configuration of the deacon to Christ the servant *permanently* identifies us and characterizes our place in the church. We stand at the altar to be impressed with the mission of the Christ so that, in imitation of Him, we may go out to bear that mission as charity. Our role at the conclusion of the Eucharist of sending the laity on a mission sweeps us up as well. May the courage that inheres in us as we answer Christ's call to orders serve us in our duty to invite the laity to fully receive their mission as well.

Do you fully receive the mystery of your call to follow the laity out of the doors of the church to animate them in service to transform culture? How are we to understand our role as animators and not initiators since the laity hold their call within the grace of baptism, not by a summons from the clergy?

Post Retreat

Deacon: A Man of Prayer, A Man of Pastoral Charity

It is my hope that this time of prayer has deepened your love of Christ and your love of the mysterious vocation he has invited you into. To step away for awhile and allow the Father to speak to you through Christ and in the Spirit is not a luxury but a necessity. The western culture of anxiety and distraction that we live in makes prayer seem like a luxury and therefore unnecessary. But, in truth, to avoid retreat time is to avoid the opportunity of *letting Christ reach you*. This avoidance of Christ assures that our vocation will simply become routine or even a burden. The vocation is from Him and so *He wants* to sustain it.

As you leave this retreat take with you any encounter you had with the living God in your memory. This gift of memory is yours to enter again and again. It is not part of a fantasy life to enter your memories of prayer or your memories of intimacy with God. Rather, to enter such is the very definition of spiritual imagination. We enter our spiritual imagination rather than fantasy because this imagination connects us to truth and reality. All fantasy leads to sadness and depression, whereas returning to times of intimacy with God in our memory, our imagination, holds with it the promise of consolation, peace and openness to ongoing conversion. It holds with it the promise of living in reality. Call upon the Spirit often, in so doing you are choosing to remain in the Presence. From such a choice astounding grace will be unleashed within the lives of the people you minister to as you *preside at the liturgy of charity*.

Personal Prayers in a Deacon's Life

Prayers Before Assisting at the Altar

Dear Lord, be with me now as I assist the priest in the Holy Eucharist. Let my mind and heart be focused upon the mystery of your Presence, the mystery of Your incredible self-gift. You want to share your body and blood with us all. Help me to know your personal love for me as I proclaim your word, intercede for the needs of your church, and distribute the precious blood which is life for us all. In my small tasks at your holy altar draw me closer to you through simplicity. Especially teach me, Lord, that you have called me to this altar so that I might be graced to share in *your own eager availability* and so serve the spiritual and corporeal needs of your church. Amen.

Prayer Before I Preach

What a marvel, that I can proclaim your word, the word which saves in its hearing. Lead me, Lord, into a love of your word above all other words that clamor to call to me each day. Fill me with your sacred silence so that I might truly seek your instruction and only yours. Enable me to teach and preach out of such silence so that the people listening may enjoy the fruit of our intimacy, an intimate love contained within and ordered by the church's continual love and protection of your holy word. Amen.

Prayer Before I Enter My Ministry

Lord, you have called me to compel others to come to the banquet. Give me the grace to show forth your beauty as I minister to the needs of your people. It is the beauty of *your love* that catches the eye of your bride. May I be a faithful friend of the bridegroom and show forth only what is most beautiful in You—selfless healing service toward those who cry out in need, pain, loneliness, confusion and doubt. In some small way, in faith, may my presence to others silence those cries. May I show all the people I minister to the way to *enduring peace and rest in the heart* of the bridegroom of the church. Amen.

Prayer for Marriage Enrichment

Lord, before I heard your call to orders, you had already given me the fullness of my heart in her, my bride. But you wanted to give me more. There is always more with you. Thank you for my wife. Thank you for the love of this woman who undergirds all that I am. She orders me to You within my call to orders. She has always pointed the way to self-dispossession and generosity. It was she who called me to maturity in love and it will be she who delights now in seeing that love mature into ecclesial ministry. What can I give to such a woman? Only You Lord. I beg you, then, to bless her beyond all telling and to see her safely into holiness and life, life abundant. Amen.

Prayer in Thanksgiving for My Ordination

As I kiss the altar of sacrifice with each Mass I assist at I thank you Lord for the call to serve your church as deacon. It was a surprise vocation, a call within a call. You moved my heart and suddenly I saw more than the success of my profession, more than my participation in civic and cultural pursuits. I saw You again, but differently. And you held out to me a new way of receiving your love and healing, a mysterious way of being saved by way of self-forgetfulness and self-emptying. Stay with me now Lord and see me through to the end of this journey. Never let me be parted from You. Thank you, in the depths of my heart, thank you for sharing your servant-heart with me. Amen.